Theosophy and the
Search for Happiness

Theosophy and the Search for Happiness

Texts by
Moon Laramie
& Annie Besant

martin firrell company
MODERN THEOSOPHY

First published in 2019 by Martin Firrell Company Ltd
10 Queen Street Place, London EC4R 1AG, United Kingdom.

ISBN 978-1-912622-04-7

Text is set in Baskerville, 12pt on 18pt.

Baskerville is a serif typeface designed in 1754 by John Baskerville
(1706–1775) in Birmingham, England. Compared to earlier typeface
designs, Baskerville increased the contrast between thick and thin
strokes. Serifs were made sharper and more tapered, and the axis of
rounded letters was placed in a more vertical position. The curved
strokes were made more circular in shape, and the characters became
more regular.

Baskerville is categorised as a transitional typeface between classical
typefaces and high contrast modern faces. Of his own typeface, John
Baskerville wrote, 'Having been an early admirer of the beauty of
letters, I became insensibly desirous of contributing to the perfection
of them. I formed to myself ideas of greater accuracy than had yet
appeared, and had endeavoured to produce a set of types according to
what I conceived to be their true proportion.'

Moon Laramie

Moon Laramie was born in London, England in July 1966. His parents were the peace activists and anti-Vietnam War agitators Jeff Laramie and Natasha 'Cherokee' Laramie. During his formative years, Moon was raised off the grid in an east London hippie collective. He studied English Literature, American Studies and creative writing at the University of Middlesex, England from 1987 to 1990. During the early 1990s he lived in southern Sweden where he worked as an English teacher with the Folk University in Gothenburg and Malmö. On returning to Britain in 1995 he settled in Manchester where he studied holistic therapies including geothermal therapy, Reiki, Indian Head Massage and meditation. He also contributed articles to a number of magazines including *Cheshire Life*. He became a Reiki master in 2005.

Moon became involved in neopaganism and was a practising Wiccan for several years. He returned to London in 2008. Between 2008 and 2015 he worked as a rights advisor for the United Nations Children's Fund. He joined the Theosophical Society in England in 2016. Moon's first book, *The Zombie Inside*, (published July 2016) explored the power and significance of thought forms. His second book, a spiritual portrait of the Swedish actress Greta Garbo, was published in September 2018. *Spirit of Garbo* quickly became an international bestseller described by Aeon Byte Gnostic Radio as 'a spiritual manual for many beneficial spiritual pursuits'.

Moon has written for a number of spiritual publications including *Kindred Spirit, The Best You* and *Watkins*. He is a regular contributor to *The Magic Happens Magazine*. He divides his time between London and Norfolk, England.

Theosophy and the
Search for Happiness
by Moon Laramie (2019)

The Nature of Happiness

It was the philanthropist Jayme Illien who first campaigned for a special day to focus on happiness. Since 2013, the United Nations International Day of Happiness has been celebrated across the world on 20 March. At its most basic, happiness might be described as the condition of feeling joy more often than sadness. 'Happy' people feel contentment more often than disappointment. Their satisfaction with life is greater than that of the average person. They are able to focus more frequently on the good. This often leads them to intense moments of bliss. These moments are what the American psychologist Abraham Maslow described as 'peak experiences'. Peak experiences are periods of euphoria when an individual enters into an effortless state, free from fear, doubt or self-criticism.

The Theosophical Society's founder, Helena Blavatsky believed that 'there can be neither happiness nor bliss without a contrasting experience of suffering and pain'.[1]

In her pamphlet *Theosophy and the Search for Happiness*, Annie Besant identifies an 'inner instinct of man, which drives him to search for happiness'.

The majority of any individual's actions, words and deeds are rooted in this search for happiness. From the development of friendships and pastimes to the choice of profession or where to settle and build a life, the decisions we make are based on a desire to be happy. Yet the human relationship with happiness is a complex one. Piecemeal moments of gratification can often appear to bring happiness. As manifestations of flesh and bone, human beings are drawn to things which give them momentary pleasures.

Henry Steele Olcott points out that 'the pleasures of the eye, the ear, the taste, touch and smell are fleeting and deceptive'.[2] Annie Besant observes that over-indulgence of sensory gratifications can result in a worn-out, bloated, unhealthy body. For each of us the body should be the mastered rather than the master.

In *Light on the Path*, Mabel Collins argues that mastery over the body is to be found by looking within rather than without. Collins urges, paradoxically, that we must 'fix the sight and hearing on that which is invisible and soundless'.[3]

The Influence of Fear

The actress Shirley MacLaine has been an enthusiastic student of theosophy. MacLaine suggests, 'To be happy you have to be willing to be compliant with not knowing.' The 'not knowing' she describes is the feeling of a lack of control over life, in essence, simply having no idea what might happen next. For many, this lack of control leads to intense feelings of uncertainty and uncertainty generates fear. Where fear resides there is no room for happiness. Professor Jon Kabat-Zinn, the founder of Massachusetts University's Stress Reduction Center, says, 'If we are honest with ourselves, most of us will have to admit that we live out our lives on an ocean of fear, much of the time trying to avoid recognising that fact.'[4] To be compliant with not knowing is to surrender control, and by surrendering, to become free from fear.

The author and founder member of the Theosophical Society, William Quan Judge suggests that living in the present can provide a potential route to this kind of freedom: 'If you will do just what lies before you without thinking about all the other things, and without troubling your mind about all the things you can't do, then it will all be different and everything will grow brighter for you.'[5]

Being present gives us back a modicum of control. If we are focused on inhabiting this moment, fear and doubt can find it hard to get in. We are empowered when we choose to focus solely on what is in front of us. We are disempowered when we allow our erratic, streaming thoughts to take over. We find ourselves surrounded by doubts and uncertainties in a world where life appears to happen to us. We can feel as if we are on a roller coaster hurtling towards an unknown destination.

Separation and Isolation

This feeling is amplified by the way in which human beings regard themselves as separate from the universe. Heavy elements like iron are only created inside exploding stars and iron is an essential component in our blood. Without it, we cannot live. We are literally made of the stuff of those exploding stars, the stuff of the universe.

In a 2015 interview in *National Geographic*, Professor Iris Schrijver of Stanford University, observes, 'Everything we are and everything in the universe and on earth originated from stardust, and it continually floats through us even today. It directly connects us to the universe, rebuilding our bodies over and again over our lifetimes.' As Abraham Maslow said, 'This is one aspect of the basic human predicament. We are simultaneously worms and gods.'[6]

It is on the material plane that we are farthest removed from the cosmic consciousness from which we were born. Living in our physical bodies, we can feel detached from the divine source, our atma, our celestial parent. It is this sense of isolation and uncertainty which contributes to feelings of fear and unhappiness. In *The Mahatma Letters*, Koot Hoomi identifies the physical plane as a place of evil where we experience an 'inherent helplessness - that of a straw violently blown hither and thither by every remorseless wind'. It is this, he argues, which 'has made unalloyed happiness on this earth an utter impossibility for the human being, whatever his chances and condition may be'.[7] According to theosophy, the after death state of Devachan is said to bring more bliss than can possibly be imagined in the apparent uncertainty of the physical world.

The Search for Truth

Theosophy is concerned with interpreting consciousness and humanity's place in the cosmos. It proposes that humanity is on an evolutionary path, ascending to the divine source from which it originally came. Ultimate reunion with this divine source brings unalloyed bliss. Any activity steering the individual towards this reunion may be seen as indicative of a movement towards happiness. Annie Besant argues that happiness is to be found by looking to the spirit and the self. Theosophy is involved with the self's search for truth. The student of theosophy becomes in essence a seeker of truth. It is the journey towards illumination that holds the key to happiness.

It is often said that ignorance is bliss but this is not always so. One only has to look at sensationalist stories in the press to recognise this. Such stories depend on ignorance to promote their twisted interpretations of the facts. Ignorance breeds fear and fear is the antithesis of happiness. Ignorance is rooted in powerlessness. Enlightenment develops the individual. It brings understanding and agency. Enlightenment lifts the individual up. Any seeker of the truth therefore finds himself on the path towards happiness. The seeking of answers lies at the heart of human experience. We look for answers to questions every day as we interpret the world and attempt to understand our place in it. The evolving human consciousness seeks to understand the nature of its own conscious being. Theosophy is rooted in an academic approach to searching for the meaning of existence. The Theosophical Society provides a forum for exploring the wisdom of the ages. The modern theosophist engages with that wisdom and uncovers what insights there are to be found. Each theosophical student is free to come to his or her own conclusions. Theosophy can be described as a path of personal discovery. Treading the theosophical path is an act of liberation which diminishes feelings of futility and fear. The individual is empowered and energised, propelled towards the ultimate goal of enlightenment and happiness.

The Fear of Death

One of the most primal of fears is the fear of the unknown. The greatest unknown of human existence is death. We know what it is like on the moon because people have gone there and come back. No one has returned from the grave. Reincarnation is a fundamental principle of theosophy. Each soul develops and refines itself through the experiences of repeated lifetimes. This is a core aspect of humanity's evolution into superlunary beings. The absolute is infinite and our connection to it means that our conscious souls are also infinite. The absolute is too great for the earthbound mind to comprehend. We see only the briefest glimpse of its true nature when we look up at a starry sky at night.

Between each incarnation there is a period of rest when the individual reunites with the divine source. We use this time to examine our life experiences and grow from them. This is our 'soul food', our sustenance for the next phase of the journey. Reincarnation, the idea that there is a path of evolution to tread, takes away the fear of death. It gives the individual soul the freedom to grow during each lifetime. Life on earth encourages us to attend to our spiritual natures. With each of our incarnations we discover more of the power we have inside. We are awakened a little further each time. Annie Besant observes, '…all happiness is divine… look through the form to the life, look through the outer vehicle to that which is within it.' Inner awakening is the only way for humanity to evolve and grow into perfected beings. When that day comes there will be no need to return to the 'school of life' on earth.

Humanity and the Absolute

There is an old saying that 'pain builds character'. In a similar way, the experience of repeated lifetimes, however painful, builds divinity. As human beings work through successive incarnations, they move along a path of spiritual evolution. The soul is refined. Humanity's brutish qualities fade and its deiform qualities grow. Revisiting the experience of life enables the individual to inch towards perfection. In its limitless infinity, the absolute holds the key to truth. Our development towards ever closer union with it, brings each of us nearer to understanding the truth it holds. Knowing we are each part of an incomprehensible power contributes to our happiness. It shows us humanity is immortal - there is no need to fear. Each of us is like a child learning and growing through trial and error. We return to walk the road again and again. Embracing the non-material is the key to development in each lifetime. One should connect to the shared human experience, recognising the existence of a universal human fellowship. Karma plays a role in any life lived. It provides feedback from the universe on progress made. It forms part of the school report in the school of life. Acts of kindness reap positive rewards. They propel the individual towards a spiritual actuality. As Helena Blavatsky points out, 'As long as we are in the body, we are subjected to pain, suffering and all the disappointing incidents occurring during life. Therefore, and to palliate this, we finally acquire knowledge which alone can afford us relief and hope of a better future.'[8]

But is there a danger in seeing life too much as a state of suffering? The smell of freshly cut grass, the feel of a warm breeze, the taste of a ripe orange - these can all produce moments of wonder. It is easy to overlook life's beauty in the quest for the intangible. The dictionary defines consciousness as 'being aware and responsive to one's surroundings'. It is much more than that. Consciousness is the part of us which is connected with the absolute. In *The Light of Asia*, Edwin Arnold refers to the beginnings of Buddha's teachings: 'Om Amitaya! measure not with words th'Immeasurable; nor sink the string of thought into the fathomless.'[9] Our sense of unbreakable connection with the infinite brings a feeling of safety and ultimately a sense joy. A relationship with the absolute is an underlying aspect of the search for happiness. As Helena Blavatsky observes, 'True Occultism is the destruction of the false idea of Self, and therefore true spiritual perfection and knowledge are nothing else but the complete identification of our finite 'selves' with the Great All. It follows, therefore, that no spiritual progress at all is possible except by and through the bulk of Humanity. It is only when the whole of Humanity has attained happiness that the individual can hope to become permanently happy - for the individual is an inseparable part of the Whole.'[10] Separation and isolation generate fear. Merging all sense of separateness into unity consciousness negates fear.

Unity Consciousness

Individuality is the foundation of personal identity. What are my tastes? What are my viewpoints? How do I like to dress? These mundane considerations are the building blocks of individuality and separateness. A person carves out a place in the world by constructing a distinct boundary between his own and other personalities. Yet behind the worldly manifestations of character and identity there is an ineradicable life force. An invisible thread connects the human psyche to the higher consciousnesses of the atma, buddhi and manas. Knowledge of this informs a sense of oneness. Unity consciousness is the foundation of Universal Brotherhood. Recognising the oneness in everything means that ultimately no one person is truly alone. Life becomes less daunting with the knowledge that everyone is a part of everyone else, a human family facing the bumps in the road together. Whatever affects me also affects a multitude of others. Events in one part of the world ripple throughout the rest along the intermingling waves of oneness and connection. Who I am is mirrored in other people and other places.

Therefore, I, or rather, we are not alone in anything. If there is a single nucleus at the heart of human experience then there is no need to feel isolated. And that single nucleus must also hold a single truth. Seeking out comparative truths among the belief systems of the world beats a path towards the ultimate single truth. It reveals the lie of separation. This is a core principle of theosophy. Theosophists are encouraged to look beyond notions of separateness to a unity consciousness hidden in plain view.

Realisation of one's own divinity brings an internal sense of harmony and self-integration. In *The Key to Theosophy*, Blavatsky comments, 'We maintain that all pain and suffering are the results of want of Harmony, and that the one terrible and only cause of the disturbance of Harmony is selfishness in some form or another.' In her *Collected Writings vol. III*, she says that 'happiness is merely a house of cards tumbling down at the first whiff; it cannot exist in reality as long as egotism reigns supreme in civilised societies. As long as intellectual progress will refuse to accept a subordinate position to ethical progress, and egotism will not give way to the Altruism preached by Gautama and the true historical Jesus (the Jesus of the pagan sanctuary, not the Christ of the Churches), happiness for all the members of humanity will remain a Utopia.'[11] Happiness is a project of global unity consciousness. Individuals are dependent on each other. Humanity is dependent on the ecosystem. The earth is dependent on the sun or solar logos. Accepting interdependency brings happiness. Working against it, doesn't. Collective solidarity moves everyone further along the path to happiness.

Impermanence as Truth

Humanity's long journey of physical transformation and spiritual evolution involves a process of constant change. For every human being, each incarnation on earth is a quickly passing moment. A much greater time is spent on the ethereal planes reviewing each life between incarnations.

If change is the truth for our spiritual existence, it must also be the same for our baser material existence. In fact, material existence is riddled with impermanence. This presents a challenge for the individual. Humans become easily addicted to repeated material pleasures. The physical body is predisposed for just such addictive behaviour. If everything remains the same, then so does the supply of those material pleasures. Change is therefore viewed with suspicion and apprehension. Such a worldview encourages lapses in development and deviations from the path of spiritual evolution.

Understanding that each of us is a divine being having a physical experience reveals the bigger picture. The body disintegrates but the spirit will go on. The cycle of life on one planet ends only to be replaced with a new cycle on another.

If anything might be described as unchanging, it is the very fact of this cycle of birth, death and rebirth on the path of cosmic evolution. Surrendering to impermanence, accepting it as a spiritual truth is part of theosophical doctrine. As Blavatsky observes, 'From a conviction of the impermanence of material happiness would result a striving after that joy which is eternal, and in which all men can share.'[12]

Universal Brotherhood

One of the objects of the Theosophical Society is the recognition of a global human brotherhood. Recognising our common humanity keeps the spirit of brotherhood alive. The goal is collective harmony, rather than the pursuit of individual happiness. In truth, individual happiness is achieved by working towards common accord. Happiness is an essential by-product of the common good. It is a lack of mutuality that results in the strife and hostility evident in the world today. Strife melts away when individuals begin to model cooperation and celebrate diversity within the framework of common humanity. Present-day humans inherited their desire for self-gratification from the ancient Atlanteans. Overcoming these tendencies is one of the great challenges facing the world. Cancer is caused by the uncontrolled growth of normal cells in the body. The growth of individualistic self-gratification might be described as the cancer of the modern age. Relentless consumerism rapes the land, depletes resources and its effects are now being felt on a global scale. The earth is suffering from a bad case of 'consumption'. One contributory factor is the lack of recognition that humanity does not stand alone. 'Brotherhood' is an inclusive rather than exclusive word. By that token it should extend to all living beings. One might term this idea as a 'commonality of being'. When overdevelopment leads to the wanton destruction of habitats and extinction of species, the human race takes another step nearer to the cliff edge. Much of modern human activity is characterised by disregard for such commonality of being. It is the 21st-century disease. As William Quan Judge observes, 'Disease is nothing more or less than the sin of separateness.'[13]

Each human consciousness is a seed of the divine consciousness. Theosophy proposes that human beings only became conscious individuals through a journey of involution. First we were sparks of the divine with no individual awareness. Individuality is attained by journeying through the kingdoms of the life waves. Each human being is drawn like a magnet back up towards reunion with the divine source. Compassion forms part of our drive to reconnect with that source. Anyone is free to nurture or neglect this inherent tendency. Nurturing it, however, leads to personal paradise.

'Compassion is no attribute. It is the law of laws - eternal harmony... a shoreless universal essence, the light of everlasting Right and fitness of all things'.[14]

William Quan Judge supports the idea that small acts of kindness hold great power: 'Act with a high motive; have kindly feelings towards all; do some little act of kindness every day and try to realise that the end of all this will be happiness and peace for all humanity. Then, a foretaste of that peace will enter your own heart. There is a bright side to life, and what makes the brightness is the love which each of us may have for humanity.'[15] Mabel Collins extends this concept, prefiguring the popular ideas of modern New Thought: 'Each man is his own absolute lawgiver, the dispenser of glory or gloom to himself; the decreer of his life, his reward, his punishment.'[16]

Happiness as a Birthright

A quest for truth lies at the heart of theosophy. Theosophists do not blindly accept proclamations from above. True epiphany comes from within. 'Therefore, the truths as to God, nature, and man's ascent to Divinity exist in man himself. The treasures of the wisdom, love and beauty of the Whole exist in the innermost recesses of man's soul. If a man will but seek rightly, he can find all truth.'[17] The divine seed is inside us all. If that seed is nurtured and grows then so does knowledge of the truth. Through its investigation of philosophy, science and religion, theosophy gives us the tools to do this. Spiritual growth is both the journey and the reward. As Annie Besant explains, 'The spiritual journey is what brings true happiness and it never diminishes, like material wealth or physical pleasure, it grows unendingly in its bounty.' It is easy to become caught up in the idea that there is something to be ashamed of in being happy. But the absolute is full of bliss and would not begrudge happiness to beings on a path of reunion with it. According to Annie Besant, 'It would indeed be well if out of the heart of every one of you could drop that ancient superstition which causes so much unhappiness, that there is something more or less wrong in being happy, that there is something more or less to be ashamed of in finding and enjoying happiness, that that old horror of Calvinism is true, that the Divine Being is pleased with sadness rather than with joy, and that He, whose innermost being is Bliss, can in any sense grudge the enjoyment of happiness by His children.' The true journey of spiritual discovery is driven by joy and happiness rather than fear. Dire warnings of hellfire and damnation are not conducive to feelings of bliss. In theosophy there is a recognition of a universal brotherhood, of a unifying truth scattered across all belief systems. Reincarnation forms part of humanity's infinite path of learning and discovery. If I am divinity experiencing material existence, I have no real need to fear death. When we realise this, we are freed from repressive notions of eternal retribution at the feet of an angry god. Theosophy, like any school of thought, cannot make a person 'happy'. But what can is the freedom from fear. The freedom to make one's own mistakes, to learn from them and spiritually evolve over many, many lifetimes.

1. Helena Petrovna Blavatsky, *Collected Writings vol. X*, Theosophical Publishing House, 1988.

2. Henry Steele Olcott, *The Life of the Buddha and its Lessons*, Theosophical Publishing House, 1912.

3. Mabel Collins, *Light on the Path*, Occult Publishing Company, 1885.

4. Jon Kabat-Zinn, *Full Catastrophe Living*, Bantam Books, 1990.

5. William Quan Judge, *Letters That Have Helped Me*, Theosophical Publishing Company, 1891.

6. Abraham Maslow, *Beyond a Psychology of Being*, Van Nostrund, 1968.

7. *The Mahatma Letters to A.P. Sinnett*, compiled by A.Trevor Barker, Rider and Company, 1923.

8. Helena Petrovna Blavatsky, *The Key to Theosophy*, Theosophical Publishing Company, 1889.

9. Edwin Arnold, *The Light of Asia*, The Useful Knowledge Publishing Company, 1879.

10. Helena Petrovna Blavatsky, *Collected Writings vol. XI*, Theosophical Publishing House, 1973.

11. Helena Petrovna Blavatsky, *Collected Writings vol. VIII*, Theosophical Publishing House, 1990.

12. Helena Petrovna Blavatsky, *Collected Writings vol. XI*, Theosophical Publishing House, 1973.

13. William Quan Judge, 'The Synthesis of Occult Science' from *The Path vol. 6 no.11*, February 1892.

14. Helena Petrovna Blavatsky, *The Voice of the Silence*, Theosophical Publishing Company, 1889.

15. William Quan Judge, *Letters That Have Helped Me*, Theosophical Publishing Company, 1891.

16. Mabel Collins, *The Idyll of the White Lotus*, John W. Lovell Company, 1890.

17. C. Jinarajadasa, *First Principles of Theosophy*, Theosophical Publishing House, 1922.

Annie Besant

Annie Besant was born in London on 1 October 1847. She was a women's rights activist, supporter of Irish independence, socialist, author and was president of the Theosophical Society from 1907 until her death in 1933. In 1867, she married Frank Besant, a clergyman, and they had two children. However, her criticism of his political and religious views led to their legal separation in 1873. She then became an active member of the National Secular Society (NSS). In 1877, she helped publish a book, *Fruits of Philosophy* by Charles Knowlton, the American birth control campaigner. The ensuing scandal put her in the public spotlight. Besant was a prolific writer and initially wrote a weekly column in *The National Reformer*. In her articles she argued for Irish home rule and a secular state in Britain. Later Besant became involved with social justice campaigns, including the London match girls strike of 1888. She was a prominent speaker for the Fabian Society and the Marxist Social Democratic Federation. In 1889, she was asked to write a review for *The Pall Mall Gazette* on *The Secret Doctrine*, the seminal work by Helena Petrovna Blavatsky. She sought an interview with its author and met

Blavatsky in Paris. Blavatsky was one of the founder members of the theosophical movement along with Henry Steele Olcott and William Quan Judge. The society was set up to promote the comparative study of philosophy, religion and science. The society described itself as 'an unsectarian body of seekers after Truth, who endeavour to promote Brotherhood and strive to serve humanity'.

Besant joined the Theosophical Society and soon became a leading lecturer and author on theosophical subjects. She published a number of books including *Thought Forms* (with C.W. Leadbeater) in 1901 and *Esoteric Christianity* in 1905. While president of the Theosophical Society, Besant was based at its headquarters in Adyar, India. She became involved in the struggle for Indian self-determination and helped launch the Home Rule League in 1914. In the late 1920s, Besant travelled to the United States with her protégé Jiddu Krishnamurti, who she hailed as the new World Teacher and incarnation of Buddha. Although Krishnamurti distanced himself from theosophy in 1929, Besant remained loyal to him. After her death, Krishnamurti, Aldous Huxley, Guido

Ferrando, and Rosalind Rajagopal built the Besant Hill School of Happy Valley in her honour. Besant's many pamphlets include *The Gospel of Christianity and the Gospel of Freethought* (1883), *Life, Death, and Immortality* (1886), *Why I Do Not Believe in God* (1887), and *Theosophy and the Search for Happiness* (1918).

Theosophy and the
Search for Happiness
by Annie Besant (1918)

The one thing in which all sentient creatures agree is that happiness is desirable, and some unconsciously, some deliberately, some under cover of another object placed ostensibly as that which is sought, engage in the continual pursuit of this one end. Everywhere man is in search of happiness; everything, in fact, around us in which sentient life is found, life capable of experiencing pleasure and pain, every such form of life is engaged in the search after happiness. Some people, with a kind of idea, apparently, that to openly seek for happiness is wrong, or in some way unworthy, cover over the fact of the search by putting forward some other end, some other aim, for life. But if we carefully examine their arguments and their conduct we find that while they may put forward what is really a means as the end at which they are aiming, the very way in which they regard that means shows that it is only an intellectual blunder that they are making in thinking that they are really seeking for that, instead of for the end to which it leads. Many of you, for instance, may have a momentary question in the mind, if you have not thought carefully over the subject before, and you may be inclined to say: 'Is it not virtue that we seek for as the end of life, rather than happiness? Do we not put before ourselves as the highest good right living, rather than bliss?' But that question, if the answer to it be analysed, will be found to be based on a misconception of the facts. Why is it that men follow virtue, save that they find in virtue an inner accord with their own being, and know that in that accord is the only means to permanent happiness? Every religion for instance, you will find, speaking of happiness on the other side of death, speaks of that happiness in connection with virtuous living, and regards it as the very crown and result of the virtue. And, truly, in that idea that happiness is the result of virtue, there is no error, for virtue is the means to happiness, the only practical means, because happiness means harmony with the divine nature, means harmony with the divine law in life, and inasmuch as nature is based on the divine existence, inasmuch as that existence manifests by law and not by arbitrary fancy or whim, it is inevitable that following that Will and the gaining of happiness shall be one and the same thing. In a universe of law, happiness must lie in union with the law, and if that law be a law of good, if it be, as it is, an expression of the divine nature, then virtue is the only road to permanent happiness, and the very test of virtuous conduct is whether it does or does not lead ultimately to happiness as its end.

For in truth as we study this question carefully we must recognise, if we be frank with ourselves, that a line of conduct which leads to misery ever-increasing, and which could only have as its end perpetual misery, is always identical with that which is against law, is that which we speak of as fundamentally vicious and not virtuous. All the consent of the world's thinking, which sees in happiness the inevitable result of virtue, is only really the instinctive prompting of man's nature, which, knowing itself divine, knows bliss to be its inevitable heritage. That God is Bliss, Brahman is Bliss, is found in Indian Scripture and in Christian Revelation. Both give the same teaching, that the very being of the divine is fundamentally happiness and not misery, joy and not sadness, bliss, in a world unending, complete and perfect. That which has sometimes veiled the reality of this as the true end of man has been that often in the course of evolution it is necessary to face a passing sorrow for a more permanent happiness, to sacrifice the lower for the higher, the transitory for the enduring; hence virtue, which means ultimately steady and permanent bliss, may sometimes for a time lead us along a path of pain or self-denial. And even then there is an inner joy, deeper than the surface pain, bearing witness to the identity of right and happiness. But that pain and self-denial we face, knowing that they are temporary, whereas the happiness is permanent; and if we find that a passing bliss gives rise to a permanent unhappiness, then at once we stamp that passing bliss as unworthy of our pursuit, and again vindicate that innermost instinct of our nature that the good and the happy are ultimately identical, that sorrow treads on the heels of evil, as the Lord Buddha said, 'as the wheels of the cart follow the heels of the ox', that, by the eternal law, that which is right means ultimately that which is bliss, while that which is evil leads as inevitably to misery; man grasps at evil, deluded by the temporary appearance, because he is ignorant instead of wise, because he is blinded by the transitory form, and the reality underneath that form is veiled from him by the lack of insight and of knowledge.

The inner instinct of man, which drives him to seek for happiness, is definitely justified alike by religion and philosophy. I have already said that all the religions of the world speak of happiness as the outcome of right doing, and the philosophies of the world - which put into intellectual form the roads along which man should intelligently travel - those philosophies either definitely, or implicitly, are all put forward as means of escaping misery. Every great school of Indian philosophy, in opening an exposition in which its principles are detailed, begins with a statement that it is the seeking to put an end to pain. That is put forward definitely as the end of the philosophy, and it is justified by the declarations that inasmuch as the supreme is bliss, as the only true wisdom is knowledge, therefore true philosophy must be the knowledge of God, and in that as inevitably is implied happiness, as light in the being of the sun.

This, then, being recognised as true, religiously and philosophically as well as practically, I propose to look with you tonight on the best way of finding happiness, so that if possible each one of us, finding in our hearts that longing, may know along which road it is best to tread in our search. For the sorrow of the world comes from the world's ignorance; the grief of the world comes from the world's delusion. Men follow what they dream will give them happiness, and over and over again it shivers in their grasp the moment they have seized it, so that human life, too often, is a succession of disappointments, and yet the ineradicable thirst for happiness still drives man along the road of this unending quest.

Now in order to know what will be happiness for us, we must know something of our own nature, must realise its wants, its demands, its cravings, and then we shall be able to discover how best those cravings may be satisfied. And in making this search, it would indeed be well if out of the heart of every one of you could drop that ancient superstition which causes so much unhappiness, that there is something more or less wrong in being happy, that there is something more or less to be ashamed of in finding and enjoying happiness, that that old horror of Calvinism is true, that the Divine Being is pleased with sadness rather than with joy, and that He, whose innermost being is Bliss, can in any sense grudge the enjoyment of happiness by His children.

Suppose, then, that we have got rid of this superstition - and I wish it went out of men's hearts as easily as the phrase can be spoken - then, looking at our own nature and its demands, we may hope to waste less time in following mistaken roads. We may hope to utilise life's experience in the best possible way, in the way in which evolution will also best be advanced. Man's nature, we have often seen, may for practical purposes be looked at as showing itself in four chief ways:

(a) We find ourselves with a physical nature surrounded by a physical world, and in this world the vehicle of our consciousness is the physical body, and all the objects which the world presents to us are objects which either attract or repel us, giving us either pleasure or pain.

(b) Then we find, looking into our nature still further, emotions, the emotional nature of man. Those have their satisfaction chiefly in the intercourse with human beings around us, in the interchange of life energies with them, the emotions being best satisfied in our intercourse with humanity. But in addition to that, those emotions are also sources of pleasure or of pain in connection with other objects in the world around us which stir them up, give life to them and expand them, or else knock roughly against them, frustrating them, denying them expansion. All the wondrous world that lies in art, in the satisfaction of the sense of beauty, all that which comes to us from the splendour of the world around us, from landscape, from colour, from light, from sound, in nature - all these are things that give satisfaction to the emotions within us, and they find their gratification in coming into touch with these harmonious vibrations in nature, to which we in turn harmoniously respond in our emotions. So that there is a second side to our nature, either to be satisfied or to be starved, which will have a very definite relation to this search after happiness, and that needs to be understood that it may be wisely guided, intelligently directed.

(c) Then we find, on looking into our nature more closely, an intellectual aspect where thought and reason, the joy of research and of knowledge, the delight in the exercise of the intelligence, of the conquest of new thought, lend happiness to life, and form the keenest enjoyments of those who have developed that aspect of their nature.

(d) And when these three ways of expressing ourselves are seen and understood - by way of the body, by way of the emotions, and by way of the intelligence - we find that all these may be satisfied, and yet in the innermost depth of our nature there may still be a craving, demanding satisfaction. It is that instinct in man that arises over and over again, reappearing perennially, however often it may be frustrated, or, for a time, submerged, the longing of the human Spirit for the divine Source whence it came, the aspiration for the perfect, the aspiration for the divine, that ineradicable thirst of man for God which nothing can extinguish, which nothing can destroy, which has embodied itself in religion after religion, which finds its satisfaction through superstition, if it cannot find its satisfaction through knowledge, which is enriched by contributions from the intelligence, from the emotions, from everything that is deepest and most essential in our life, the very Self in us, that yearns after the satisfaction of union with the SELF in all; it is the craving of man to find himself in the One as well as in the many, to find that peace which can never be found in the changing conditions around us, the peace, the stability, the permanence, which are only in the Self, the Self which is divine in its origin, and only finds satisfaction in conscious union with the divine. Human restlessness everywhere eloquently speaks of man's lack of final satisfaction until that peace is found, and in the course of evolution, in the course of our growth, we find that everything fails us save that alone, that however long aught else may last, brought from any other source, in the end it breaks into pieces in our hands, and we are left empty where we had dreamed of fullness.

Very great demands, then, arise for satisfaction from human nature. Sometimes these demands conflict the one with the other, and hence the confused thought of man regarding happiness and right. But perfect happiness would satisfy everything which exists in man's complex nature, everything in him which is permanent, which expresses itself in many ways. Passing manifestations - those may perish and leave us unhappy, but that which is fundamental in our nature, that must be satisfied, else happiness cannot be. Now, if we look at the men around us, the vast majority, whatever may be their theories of life, we see, by observation, they are seeking their objects of happiness on the material plane. I am speaking of a matter of dry fact, which every one of you can verify by observation. Most of those around us seek some satisfaction of the body, however much for a while it may be veiled. Wealth, perhaps, more than any one thing, is sought by men in all ages, under all conditions of civilisation, but wealth is not sought for itself, not even in the cases which show that strange twist in human nature which identifies the means with the end, giving us the phenomenon of the miser, who cares for wealth for itself, as he says, and not for the command which it gives over objects that are seen as yielding pleasure. Wealth is followed by people constantly because of the command that it gives over material objects, not for itself but for the power that lies within it - for that reason men are ever seeking after wealth.

Now the question must at once arise, especially for the young who have their lives before them to plan out and to direct: Is it the path of a wise man, looked at intellectually, to turn the chief endeavours of his life, the chief efforts of his intelligence, the chief strain of his powers, to the mere gathering of anything which will only give satisfaction to the most passing part of his nature? Does happiness really lie in multiplying the wants of the body, or in diminishing them? Along the line of luxury, or along the side of frugality? Along the side of increasing the demands of the body, or along the side of narrowing those demands to the greatest possible extent? There is a question worth thinking over at leisure, worth weighing, analysing and answering. For on the answer to that depends practically the guidance of your life; and on the answer of the majority amongst you depends also the future of the nation. This is one of the great problems that lie before every nation at the present time - whether it tends to pursue the path of material luxury, the multiplication of material wants, seeking more and more gratification by the creation of artificial wants, in luxury, in show, in ever-increasing gratification of ever-increasing material demands. Is it along that road that happiness is to be found either for the individual or for the nation?

Other nations in the past have asked that question, and have answered that happiness is to be sought in luxury, in the multiplication of wants and in their gratification; and the end of it, for every such nation, has been death, not life. Look back in history, and you will find that history is strewn with the wrecks of civilisations, and, if you study those civilisations, you will find that they were ever civilisations that sought increasing luxury of the body, increasing sensual gratification, increasing pleasures in connection with the physical, material life. We are beginning to go - nay, we have been going for a considerable time - along this well-trodden path which so many nations have trodden before us, and, by the madness which possesses each nation in turn, as it occupies the stage of the world, we think that while other nations have perished along that road, we and we only shall escape, that though other civilisations have perished by luxury, ours shall not thus perish, that though other civilisations have grown rotten by luxury, ours will remain vigorous and strong; we are blind to the signs of decadence around us, shown in our art, shown in our literature, as well as in the unbridled luxury of the wealthy, in the ever-increasing search for pleasures that perish in the using; our national civilisation is walking along the road on which history has written but a single word and that word an epitaph: 'To the memory of a perished nation, the tombstone of a vanished civilisation!'

Why is death written on all those individuals or nations who seek in the life of the body, however refined, happiness which cannot lie there? The reason is not far to seek. The body, first of all, is a thing of habit, and its happiness is measured, not by the pleasures that you give it, but by the cravings that remain unsatisfied. The happiness of the body quickly wears itself out. The body is so much a creature of habit that, when it has enjoyed anything for a short time, that thing loses its power to give pleasure. Who are the people who enjoy wealth? Not those who are born wealthy, nor even those who long have possessed wealth. The pleasures of wealth are really felt by those who have suffered poverty and who have the power of gratifying cravings that have long been demanding satisfaction. But when these are satisfied, when the satisfaction has become habitual, then weariness takes the place of pleasure and satiety the place of satisfaction. It is a mark of all physical enjoyments that as they are exercised they gradually lose the power to give pleasure, and that, a little later, disgust and weariness succeed. In all cases of physical enjoyment the limit of enjoyment is narrow, and when that limit is overpassed, a stronger and stronger stimulus is needed to give pleasure, and when that stronger and stronger stimulus is supplied, then the organ by which the pleasure is felt wears out by the very exertion of taking it, and so disgust treads on the heels of pleasure and weariness on the heels of enjoyment.

How much better, then, knowing that by study, rather to limit the wants of the body than to increase them; for here again habit stands true and firm. Limit the satisfactions of the body, and the body becomes as happy in the midst of the frugal living as it ever was in the midst of luxurious enjoyment, finds itself as contented with simplicity as with luxury, with sufficiency as with superfluity.

I am not speaking of that pain which no human being in a properly organised society should endure, the pain of starvation, of the absolute lack of those necessities of life which preserve the health of the body. Health is necessary to physical happiness, and every man, woman, and child should be under conditions where health is possible, where health is attainable, and where only his own fault brings about the misery of bodily disease, of bodily weakness; the present social miseries are inevitable conditions, which will gradually disappear when men have learned that real happiness does not lie in the physical world.

Now that brings me to a point that is of moment to every one of us. All physical things perish in the using, and therefore are sources of combat and struggle. Where a nation is continually seeking enjoyment, it consumes with every hour of pleasure, it destroys with every satisfaction of its craving, and as, in physical nature, you can multiply desires much faster than you can multiply the objects of desire, the inevitable result is that where one class is luxurious another class is deprived of the ordinary comforts of existence, and that where, at one pole, there is an over-wealthy and luxurious class, at the other there is the misery of poverty and of disease. That is the mark of physical gratification that we cannot escape. We cannot produce as fast as we are able to consume. There might be enough produced to give to all the satisfaction of reasonable bodily demands, to make all bodies healthy and physically happy; there never can be enough produced by human labour to give ever-increasing luxury to some without contest and misery amongst those who produce for the few. That is the inevitable truth, the non-recognition of which has brought about the perishing of the civilisations of which I spoke; for unbridled luxury on the one side means misery upon the other, and as long as men place their happiness in the enjoyment of things that perish in the using, so long will society be a field of struggle, a field of battle; for each man, fearing his share will be insufficient, strives to take more than he has need of at the moment, in order to provide for the feared necessities of the future. Hence the young man and the young woman who choose wisely will begin by choosing the physically simple, rather than the physically luxurious life, training the body and disciplining it, instead of pampering it and giving it more than it needs. For the body is an admirable servant, but it is an intolerable tyrant as a master, and you may see the picture of what the body becomes, when it is made master instead of servant, if you look at the worn-out sensualist, the worn-out voluptuary. There is the Nemesis of nature for placing happiness in the body that perishes, instead of in those higher regions of human nature which give to man a happiness other than that of the body.

Pass on to the next department of our nature, and see how far happiness may be found in the gratification of the emotions. Here, if the emotions that are gratified are wisely chosen, far more of value will come into the life, far more growth in humanity, far more progress in evolution. Choose wisely the emotions which you gratify, and they will lift you upwards instead of dragging you down. Make as your rule, in choosing the emotions that are to be gratified, that they shall be those that can be gratified without injury to others, those the gratification of which tends to the happiness of all and not to your own alone, which enable you to add more and more to the joy of the world, which culture in you all that is delicate, refined and comparatively permanent, rather than the emotions which will be gratified along the lower lines of human evolution. Remember, especially if you are dealing with the young, that on the tastes that you develop on the emotional side will largely depend the line of evolution along which the soul will pass, the way in which it will climb out of evil and be attracted to the good.

Take a youth entering into life, in whom physical health is strong, where the demands of the body are violent, and see how unwise is the guidance to which he is too often subjected, how unreasonable the demands that too often are made upon him. If we want to help the young amongst us, boys and girls alike, to grow and develop and have happiness in life, we ought to use all the loftier emotions to raise them out of finding enjoyment in the exercise of the lower. If you find a youth inclined to seek pleasure in vicious indulgences, inclined to give way to the cravings of the lower nature, the way to meet him is not by rebuke, not by anger, not by contempt, but by placing within his reach pleasures that refine instead of pleasures that degrade, pleasures that elevate instead of pleasures that lower. You should use all art, all beauty, all that attracts the growing, developing nature, in order to lead him gently along the road where higher and nobler satisfaction may be found; not by insisting on asceticism, but by training in temperance, will you gradually refine the natures that you have to deal with and lift them above the possibility of temptation. The harm that is over and over again done to youthful natures is in insisting on an unwise asceticism, in pressing on them that which does not attract, and denying them everything that does; whereas when you find the nature reaching out, your duty is to try and satisfy it by gratifying the highest demands in it, and so gradually letting the lower ones be starved out; one reason why, so often, the sons and daughters of religious families turn out wilder and worse than the children of men and women of the world is because the nature has been repressed instead of guided, has been frustrated instead of developed, has been taught to look on all joy as more or less evil and dangerous; hence, as the young will at all risks enjoy, pleasure is grasped at without discrimination, and seized without knowledge. The love of joy, the love of beauty, these are the outstretching hands of the soul, groping after the divine Beauty and the divine Bliss. It is ignorance that makes them grasp in the wrong direction. It is ignorance that makes them choose the paths that lead to sorrow. Guide them, but do not deny them happiness. Help them, do not frustrate their longings; and use their love of beauty and joy to lift them some steps along the path of evolution, teaching them to seek their pleasures in the relatively permanent more than in the transitory, in that which spreads happiness around them instead of that which brings sorrow and degradation in its wake.

The emotions, then, wisely dealt with, are part of that side of our nature which may show us the way to happiness. Wisely dealt with, I say, for in this comes the profound lesson, that love, which is the deepest of the emotions, the gratification of which gives the most permanent delights, must be purified from selfishness, and must more and more find its satisfaction in what it gives, rather than in what it takes. For the love that gives lifts us to the spiritual nature, while the love that takes draws us down the ladder of evolution, and man's place in evolution may be judged by that which is the dominant element in his love, the giving or the taking element. All the sorrow of life comes out of the longing to grasp, to take, to monopolise for ourselves. All its joy - and that joy grows with our growing - lies in its giving, lies in its yielding itself, lies in its pouring out itself and finding happiness in the joy which it creates; that is the love which is divine, which lifts us, which is essentially spiritual, and therefore lasting in its nature; you may use your emotions to lead up to that greatest of possessions, a love which, finding bliss in spreading happiness, can never be taken away from us, can never be broken by any change of circumstances or by any shock of grief.

So also as we go on with our study, we find in the gratification of the intellect another of those lines where the search for happiness will bring an ever-growing gratification. Hard sometimes in the early stages, meaning self-denial and pain which is passing, rewarded with how much happiness that is lasting! You will see, if you analyse the line along which we are going, that more and more happiness is secured as the happiness is based on our own character and nature, and not on the things that surround us, that our happiness grows as we find it in the development of the life within us and not in the grasping at the things around us. To put a startling contrast between the man who has chosen the physical and the man who has chosen the emotional and the intellectual: you may take from the one all the circumstances that gave him happiness, and he lies miserable and wretched, because his life was outside him instead of within; whereas the man who has put his happiness in the growth and the purification and development of the emotions and the intellect, he may be stripped of everything and still remain content and happy, for his life is within him, his strength is within him. The more internal the happiness the more lasting it is in its nature.

But that only leads us on to the one final answer, which is to be the crown of human evolution, which is to give the uttermost satisfaction to the whole nature. Man's true happiness ultimately lies beyond even intellect and emotion, beyond all that art and beauty can do for us, beyond all that literature and genius can bestow upon us, great as are those royal gifts from those who illuminate the world. Far beyond those gratifications lie the pleasures of the spiritual nature, that joy of the innermost essence of the Self, that is ever-increasing not diminishing, that grows with exercise instead of lessening. I put on the physical, as the mark of the folly of therein finding happiness, that it perished in the using, was consumed in the enjoying; but with the development of the higher emotions, with the development of the powers of the intelligence, and still more with the unfolding of the spiritual nature, of which these are the reflected aspects, happiness grows and increases with use, and the more we consume the more we have left. That is true of the intellect. It never gives rise to struggle between man and man, when turned towards pure intelligence. There never can be too many works of genius; there never can be too many triumphs of beauty. The more these powers are exercised, the happier is the world by their results. If I learn a thing, I have first the joy of learning, then the joy of extended vision which is the result of that exercise of the intelligence, then the joy of sharing it with all those who are around me; and the more I give the more I have to give; for it is the glory of the intelligence that the more it gives the more it has to share, the more it expends itself the richer it becomes. If I teach you a truth, I am not the poorer, because you have that truth as well as I; nay, I am the richer, not only because my knowledge is yours, but also because, in the sharing, I know the truth better than I knew it before I taught it. In the very teaching comes added vision; in the very sharing comes added knowledge; in the very giving comes increase of the wealth; to spread knowledge blesses those who give it, still more perhaps than the one who receives it; so that in the giving you grow richer, and the joy is ever increasing instead of lessening by the gift.

Now, as that is realised, and as we realise still further that in the spiritual world all this is a thousandfold increased, then indeed we see the direction in which our thoughts, our efforts, should be turned, if we would have happiness in life. Nothing makes happiness permanent save the unfolding of the spiritual nature within us. Everything else may fail us; this can fail us never. Beauty - that may fail us; we may lose the power to perceive it. Intelligence - that may fail us; ever the grave closes over us, for it cannot express itself here when its physical organ is decayed; but the life of

the Spirit is ever-growing, ever-increasing it knows
no limitation, it knows no frustration, it knows no
possibility of loss or destruction. As that increases,
we find that all that is permanent in the emotions,
all that is permanent in the intelligence, is really part
of the spiritual life, the reflection of the eternal
beauty and knowledge which are of the very essence
of happiness. It is as though the divine Father of life
coaxed His children along the road of evolution by
placing before them the flowers of emotion and the
flowers of intelligence, that they may tread the road
that leads upwards to the Self. For we find, as we
begin to understand, that all that we knew of joy in
the emotions was really a reflection from the perfect
beauty of the Self; that it was not in its essence
fleeting, that it was not in its essence perishable, that
it was and is part of the eternal Beauty, part of the
eternal Bliss. If we lose here the objects of our
emotions, so that life seems withered of its joy, then,
as the Spirit unfolds, we find that we are not
separated from them, and that the joy of the
emotion between us belongs to the lasting element
and not to the temporary, that love is spiritual in its
essence, not even emotional in its root, and that they

come back to us dearer a thousandfold as the spiritual nature unfolds. And if with regard to the intelligence the physical organ weakens, then we find, as the spiritual nature unfolds, that the intelligence can work in other regions, can work in other spheres, can work in loftier worlds. For the intelligence is also of the being of the Self, is also part of our essential nature, and in unfolding the Spirit, we develop all that is permanent in us, all that, in its passing reflections, has been to us the source of real joy.

There, then, is the crown of the search for happiness: we find it in the Spirit, we find it in the Self, we find that it is lasting and not transitory, and that neither birth nor death can wrench it out of our hands. If you are sorrowful, it is because the passing has blinded your eyes to the eternal. If you are sorrowful, it is because you are grasping the reflection in the lower worlds instead of the reality in the higher. For know this of a surety, that as there is only One Life in the universe and that Life divine, infinite joy and knowledge and existence rest in that Life, which is ours merely because we live; that Life is Wisdom, that Life is Bliss, that Life is Eternity, and the Spirit in us is of the essence of that Life. All that is joyous has its joy in that Life, and only the blinding veil of ignorance here makes joy turn into pain. It is written in an Indian scripture that wherever you find the Divine Life there is joy; wherever you find joy, there a ray of the Divine Life is beaming; only, in our ignorance, we take the joy in vessels which are brittle, and when the vessels break, we have pain instead of peace.

Realise that all happiness is divine, and then you will know where to hold, and where to let go. Then you will have the test-stone by which is shown the difference between the life which is joy, and the form which is often the source and the cause of pain. Look through the form to the life; look through the outer vehicle to that which is within it; in your friends, in your daily circumstances, in everything around you, look through that which appears to the eye to that which the Spirit knows and feels. Then in the midst of earthly troubles, your joy shall be secure; then in the midst of loss, your wealth shall be safe; then in the midst of trouble, your peace shall be unruffled; in the midst of storm, calm shall remain with you. Build on the permanent, the eternal, the real, and none can touch the joy within you nor change it into sorrow.

Have the peace of the heart, and all else may fail you, and you remain content. And remember that this happiness is only yours as you help others to find it; that your life can only know the joy of the Eternal as you feel your life to be one with all lives around you; and that you may never purchase your own happiness by pain to 'the meanest thing that breathes'.

CPSIA information can be obtained
at www.ICGtesting.com
Printed in the USA
BVHW031051050619
550220BV00005B/680/P

9 781912 622047